This book belongs to:

Copyright © 2022 by Aminata Coote

All rights reserved. No part of this publication may be reproduced, distributed, or transmitted in any form or by any means, including photocopying, recording, or other electronic or mechanical methods, without the prior written permission of the publisher, except in the case of brief quotations embodied in critical reviews and certain other noncommercial uses permitted by copyright law. For permission requests: Aminata@hebrews12endurance.com.

Names: Coote, Aminata (Christian blogger) author

Title: Affirmations for Christian Women: Biblical Affirmations for Spiritual and Emotional Self-Care / Aminata Coote

Identifiers: 979-8-4199-4-8501
Subjects: Biblical References—Quotations—Self-Help—Affirmations

Cover design by Aminata Coote

AFFIRMATIONS
for Christian WOMEN

Biblical Affirmations for Spiritual
and Emotional Self-Care

AMINATA COOTE

Also by Aminata Coote

How To Find Your Gratitude Attitude
Face Your Fears: Choose Faith Over Fear
7 Lessons on Endurance from Hebrews 12:1-2
Through God's Eyes: Marriage Lessons for Women
Royal: Life Lessons from the Book of Esther
Draw Closer 52 Week Devotional Journal
Draw Closer 52 Week Companion Journal
The Book of Haggai Bible Study Workbook
Bible Study Workbook on the Book of Ezra
Affirmations for Christian Women: Biblical Affirmations for Spiritual and Emotional Self-Care (Pocket-Sized Edition)

Dedication

To Denise, if it had not been for you, this book wouldn't have been written. Thank you for always encouraging me to do the next thing.

Table of Contents

Introduction	11
What are Positive Affirmations?	15
When to Use Affirmations and How	27
How to Use the Bible Affirmations in This Book	31
Bible Affirmations for Identity	35
Biblical Affirmations for Spiritual Warfare	41
Biblical Affirmations for Self-Esteem	47
Affirmations for Courage	53
Biblical Affirmations for Success	59
Biblical Affirmations When You Feel Ashamed	65
Biblical Affirmations for Anxiety	71
Affirmations for Perseverance	77
Affirmations for Leadership	83
Affirmations for Self-Control	89
Affirmations to Encourage Your Faith	95
Affirmations for Healing/Health	101
Choose the Positive	107
About the Author	111

God is within me, I shall not fail.

Psalm 46:5

Introduction

Have you gotten into the habit of negative self-talk? Positive words of affirmation are important for your emotional health. We all need encouragement and emotional support, especially in recent years.

The past two years have been rough and many persons have found themselves cut off from their usual sources of encouragement and empowerment. So what do we do next? Do we just curl up into a ball and lament the loss of what we consider normal?

No, my sister, we do not. We get up and fight. We snatch back our empowerment from the enemy because you see, as Christian women we have to remember that we're not wrestling against flesh and blood, no, we are fighting against spiritual enemies (Ephesians 6:12).

The enemy wants to destroy Jehovah's people and he's not afraid to get inside our heads to do it. He will use our fears, disappointment, and the words of people around us to beat us down.

The key to success is to remember that in this fight, He who is within us is greater than he who seeks to destroy us (1 John 4:4). Stay strong, my sister, and speak life and truth into your circumstances.

This is not an ordinary affirmation book where we try to build up ourselves using the power of *our* words. No, we are using the words of our Creator, Almighty God to affirm us where we are weak.

The affirmations in this book are Bible-based and will point you back to Christ. Each affirmation will include the reference to a passage of Scripture. I encourage you to read the verse in your Bible, memorize it, or write it on a piece of paper...anything. Do something to remind yourself that the Word of Jehovah is living and active and sharper than a two-edged sword (Hebrews 4:12).

Jehovah has plans for my life.

Jeremiah 29:11

One

What are Positive Affirmations?

We could all use a little encouragement. As the Jamaican proverb goes, "encouragement sweetens labor" giving us the drive we need to push a little more towards our goals. Unfortunately, encouragement from external forces is sometimes few and far between.

As women, we need affirmations and encouragement so we can speak into the lives of others. We have to build ourselves up before we can nurture and build up others.

So what does it mean to affirm? The Oxford Dictionary defines affirmation as:

- the action or process of affirming something
- emotional support or encouragement.

To affirm something is to say it publicly or boldly. A personal affirmation is something positive we tell ourselves. Usually, it is a truth that we *want* to believe.

Why Are Positive Affirmations Important?

Research has shown that a good portion of our thoughts is negative (maybe as much as 70%). Not only that, but we tend to have the same negative thoughts repeatedly[1].

Negative thoughts weigh us down and we can't afford to give the enemy any weapons to use against us. The apostle Paul tells us that we should capture every thought and make it obedient to Christ (2 Corinthians 10:5).

---

[1] How Negative is Your "Mental Chatter"?, Psychology Today, https://www.psychologytoday.com/us/blog/sapient-nature/201310/how-negative-is-your-mental-chatter

Examples of Positive Affirmations for Women

But what are some good positive affirmations? A positive affirmation should emphasize something good about the speaker. It should generate courage and motivate you to accomplish your task.

A positive affirmation is usually in the first person singular and is meant to be spoken aloud. Something about hearing words does more to cement it in our thoughts than just reading them.

Here are some examples of good positive affirmations for women:

- ♥ I am beautiful.

- ♥ My worth is not defined by anyone.

Two

When to Use Affirmations and How

Affirmations are helpful when you want to change your mindset about something. When we're feeling anxious, our natural tendency is to focus on our anxiety or the thing that is causing us to feel anxious. On the other hand, if you were to claim the peace you want to feel, you'll eventually feel calmer. But you may have to claim that peace over and over again.

One of my favorite verses to focus on when I'm anxious is Isaiah 26:3. I personalize the verse and say it over and over again until my anxiety recedes. I repeat this verse every time I start to feel anxious again.

You may say your affirmations at the beginning of your day. Or you may choose to say them before bedtime or only when you feel as if you need them. Whatever you decide to do, commit to it. The mindset that you're trying to shift didn't begin in a single day; it won't change in a single day either.

Be consistent and know that enemy doesn't want you to change your mindset. He doesn't want you to do anything that will reduce his power over you. Jehovah has already given you the victory; you just need to claim it.

Three

How to Use the Bible Affirmations in This Book

It's important for us to base our beliefs on the truth of Jehovah's Word. All of the Bible affirmations will include the Scripture reference. The Bible is living and active (Hebrews 4:12) so you may find that one verse has multiple applications.

Use the table of contents to identify the mindset you'd like to shift. Before you read the affirmations, ask yourself the questions below:

♥ What are some signs that you're struggling with this particular mindset?

♥ What triggered it?

♥ What is at the root cause of this mindset?

Read the affirmations related to that mindset. Where possible, read the affirmations aloud so that you can also hear them.

If time permits, read the related Bible verse in its context and journal how you feel about it. Highlight them. Color them. Write them in your journal. Memorize them. Do something to interact with Jehovah's Word so the truth can become part of your subconscious.

I also encourage you to write down anything the Holy Spirit reveals to you in a journal or notebook so you can go back to the lessons over and over again.

As you read and study your Bible, I encourage you to make your own list of positive affirmations. But making a list is not enough. Spend a few moments each day to speak those truths over your life. The enemy is out to get you, but you can resist him if you go into battle wearing the full armor of God (Ephesians 6:10-18).

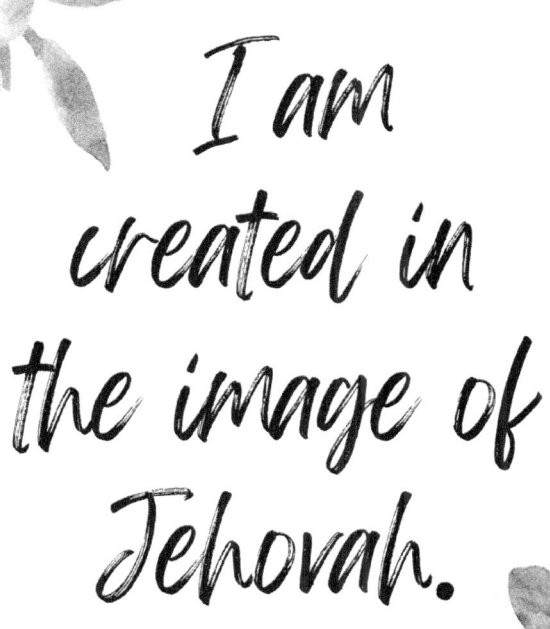

I am created in the image of Jehovah.

Genesis 1:27

Four

Bible Affirmations for Identity

Because it's important for us to speak truth over our lives, here are some positive words of affirmations that are based on what Jehovah says about us. When we begin our Bible affirmations with the phrase "I am" it's a way of claiming them as ours and making them personal.

- ♥ I am created in the image of Jehovah. Genesis 1:27

- ♥ I am chosen by Jehovah. 1 Peter 2:9

- ♥ I am Jehovah's workmanship. Ephesians 2:10

- ♥ I am a child of Jehovah. John 1:12
- ♥ Jehovah loves me with an everlasting love. Jeremiah 31:3

♥ I am fearfully and wonderfully made by my Creator. Psalm 139:13-14

♥ I am His. Jehovah calls me by name. Isaiah 43:1

♥ Jehovah is my Father. Romans 8:15

♥ I am loved by Jehovah. 1 John 3:1

♥ Christ loves me enough to die for me. Romans 5:8

♥ My life is hidden with Christ in Jehovah. Colossians 3:3

♥ My citizenship is in heaven because of Christ Jesus. Philippians 3:20

My Affirmations

I am a conqueror through Jesus Christ.

Romans 8:37

Five

Biblical Affirmations for Spiritual Warfare

As Christian women, we should remember that we're involved in a spiritual battle. The affirmations in this section remind you that you have powerful weapons with which to fight the enemy.

♥ I will put on the whole armor of Jehovah. Ephesians 6:11

♥ Jehovah has given me weapons of warfare to destroy strongholds. 2 Corinthians 10:3-5

♥ El-Elyon is my refuge and fortress. I dwell in the shadow of His wings. Psalm 91:1-16

♥ Jehovah will defeat all the enemies that rise up before me. Deuteronomy 28:7

♥ I am a servant of Jehovah. I am victorious over every weapon formed against me. Isaiah 54:17

♥ I am an overcomer because He who is within me is greater than he who within the world. 1 John 4:4

♥ All things are possible with Jehovah. Luke 1:37

♥ Jehovah is with me. I will not be overwhelmed. Isaiah 43:2

♥ I am strong in the Lord. Ephesians 6:10

♥ Jehovah gives me victory through Jesus Christ. 1 Corinthians 15:57

♥ I claim victory over my enemies because the Lord fights my battles. Deuteronomy 20:4

♥ Jehovah is within me, I shall not fail. Psalm 46:5

My Affirmations

I am a crown of beauty in Jehovah's hand.

Isaiah 62:3

Six

Biblical Affirmations for Self-Esteem

A person's self-esteem is all about what they think about themselves. Do they have confidence in their abilities? Do they know their own worth? Do they respect themselves? The enemy likes to chip away at our self-esteem and replace what Jehovah says about us with lies. We can regain that power when we choose to repeat biblical affirmations to improve our self-esteem.

Here are some Bible affirmations you can try:

♥ I am strong and courageous because the Lord is with me wherever I go. Joshua 1:9

♥ I am precious in Jehovah's eyes. Isaiah 43:4

♥ I was bought with a price. 1 Corinthians 6:20

♥ I can do all things through Christ who strengthens me Philippians 4:13

♥ I am a crown of beauty in Jehovah's hand. I am a diadem[2] in His hand. Isaiah 62:3

♥ I am a new creation in Christ. 2 Corinthians 5:17

♥ I am a child of Jehovah, a fellow-heir of His inheritance with Christ. Romans 8:16-17

♥ Jehovah loves me with an everlasting love. Jeremiah 31:3

♥ I am fearfully and wonderfully made. Jehovah knit me together in my mother's womb. Psalm 139:13-14

♥ I am Jehovah's masterpiece, created in Christ to do good works. Ephesians 2:10

♥ I am so valuable to Jehovah, He's numbered every hair on my head. Luke 12:7

♥ I am worthy of being cherished, loved, respected because I'm loved by Jehovah. John 3:16

---

[2] A diadem is a jewelled crown or headband worn as a symbol of sovereignty.

My Affirmations

I am strong in the Lord.

Ephesians 6:10

Seven

Affirmations for Courage

The Bible tells us in 2 Timothy 1:7 that Jehovah did not give us a spirit of fear. It therefore means that our fear comes from somewhere else. If you read Genesis 3, you'll see that fear was one of the emotions man began to experience after sin (Genesis 3:9-10).

The affirmations in this section remind you that your courage is found in Jehovah.

♥ Jehovah is near to me. I can call on Him to help me. Psalm 145:18

♥ I am not afraid. Jehovah has promised never to leave me nor forsake me. Deuteronomy 31:6

♥ Jehovah is mighty to save. Zephaniah 3:17

♥ Jehovah has not given me a spirit of fear but of love and of power and a sound mind. 2 Timothy 1:7

♥ I am not afraid because the Lord is my helper. What can man do to me? Hebrews 13:6

♥ I am a conqueror through Jesus Christ. Romans 8:37

♥ I am as bold as a lion through Christ. Proverbs 28:1

♥ The Holy Spirit helps me when I am weak. Romans 8:26

♥ I am strong and courageous because the Lord is with me wherever I go. Joshua 1:9

♥ My heart is firm. I trust in the Lord. Psalm 112:7

My Affirmations

I am the head and not the tail.

Deuteronomy 28:13

Eight

Biblical Affirmations for Success

Solomon, the wisest man who ever lived, admitted that death and life are in the power of the tongue (Proverbs 18:21). Our positive words have the ability to improve our lives or to destroy us from the inside out. We can greatly increase our possibility of success when we choose to remain positive.

One way to do this is to choose to speak Bible affirmations over our projects and ourselves.

♥ I am blessed because I trust Jehovah. Jeremiah 17:7

♥ Jehovah has laid out a path before me and I can trust Him. Proverbs 3:5-6

♥ Jehovah has given me everything I need to get through this. 1 Corinthians 10:13

♥ Jehovah is at my right hand, I will not be shaken. Psalm 16:8

♥ Jehovah has blessed me with everything I need to succeed. 2 Corinthians 9:8

♥ Jehovah has made me the head and not the tail. Deuteronomy 28:13

♥ Jehovah's favor is on me and He will establish the work of my hands. Psalm 90:17

♥ I am a light because of Christ and I will walk as a child of light. Ephesians 5:8

♥ Nothing is impossible with Jehovah. Luke 1:37

♥ Jehovah has plans for my life. He wants to give me hope and a future. Jeremiah 29:11

♥ I am part of a chosen generation, a royal priesthood, and a holy nation. I will proclaim the excellencies of Jehovah. 1 Peter 2:9

My Affirmations

Nine

Biblical Affirmations When You Feel Ashamed

Shame is another emotion humanity experienced after The Fall (Genesis 3:9-10). It is one the enemy uses with ferocity because he knows that shame, like fear, can have a crippling effect. He often reminds us of sins that we've already repented of and been forgiven for as a way to show that we're not worthy of Jehovah's love.

Use the affirmations in this section as a reminder that the power of Jehovah's forgiveness releases us from all fear.

♥	I am free from death and sin in Christ Jesus. Romans 8:2

♥	I have the gift of eternal life because I believe in Jesus Christ. Romans 6:23

♥	My sins are forgiven because Jehovah is faithful. 1 John 1:9

♥	I am not condemned because I am in Christ. Romans 8:1

♥ I have been made righteous in the sight of Jehovah through Jesus Christ. Romans 5:1

♥ The truth of Jesus Christ has set me free. John 8:32

♥ My body is the temple of the Holy Spirit who lives in me. 1 Corinthians 6:19-20

♥ I have been redeemed through the blood of Jesus. Colossians 1:13-14

♥ I am not ashamed of the gospel of Jesus Christ. Romans 1:16-17

♥ I am a new person in Christ. 2 Corinthians 5:17

♥ Christ has set me free. Galatians 5:1

My Affirmations

The Lord sustains me.

Psalm 41:3

Ten

Biblical Affirmations for Anxiety

Anxious thoughts can cause us to question our identity in Christ. They make us feel as if our worlds are out of control and there's nothing we can do. But we don't have to do anything, dear sister. Christ has overcome the world for us. He invites us to bring our cares to Him and He will give us rest (Matthew 11:28-30).

- ♥ Perfect peace belongs to me when I fix my mind on Christ. Isaiah 26:3

- ♥ I can trust Jehovah to take care of what worries me. Philippians 4:6

- ♥ I have joy in the Lord. He is my strength. Nehemiah 8:10

- ♥ Jehovah is in control. I am in His hands. Job 12:10

♥ I am not afraid. Jehovah strengthens me. He upholds me with His righteous right hand. Isaiah 41:10

♥ I have peace in Christ. He overcame the world for me. John 16:33

♥ Jesus Christ has given me peace. John 14:27

♥ I cast all my anxieties on Jesus because He cares for me. 1 Peter 5:7

♥ The peace of Jehovah protects my heart. Philippians 4:7

♥ Jehovah has blessed me with peace. Psalm 29:11

♥ When I am afraid, I put my trust in you. Psalm 56:3

♥ The Lord delivers me from all my fears. Psalm 34:4

My Affirmations

I will endure.

James 1:2

Eleven

Affirmations for Perseverance

One of the areas where we fail is endurance. As women of God, we suffer trials and tribulations and sometimes we want to give up. But we must hold on and persevere to the end. When you feel as though your ability to endure is being tested, use the affirmations in this section to build up your faith. You can do it, my sister. You can endure.

♥ I will wait on the Lord and He will renew my strength. I will run and not be weary; I will walk and not faint. Isaiah 40:31

♥ I will endure. This trial will produce steadfastness. James 1:2-4

♥ I will run to obtain the prize that Jehovah has promised. 1 Corinthians 9:24

♥ I will not lose heart. 2 Corinthians 4:16-18

♥ I am not being tempted beyond my ability to endure. Jehovah is faithful. He's already made a way for me to escape the temptation. 1 Corinthians 10:13

♥ I will run with endurance the race set before me. Hebrews 12:1

♥ I will remain steadfast under trial. I will receive the crown of life that Jehovah has promised to those who love Him. James 1:12

♥ I will not grow weary. I will reap a reward if I don't give up. Galatians 6:9

♥ I will fight the good fight. I will finish the race. I will keep the faith. 2 Timothy 4:7

♥ Jehovah is good. His steadfast love endures forever. Psalm 100:5

My Affirmations

I am a good example to others.

1 Timothy 4:12

Twelve

Affirmations for Leadership

Every woman in the family of God is called to leadership. We are leaders in the home, at school, church, work, or wherever we find ourselves. It is therefore important for us to exhibit the traits of a good leader. The affirmations in this section will remind us of the biblical standards of leadership.

♥ I am an example to others in speech, conduct, love, faith, and purity. 1 Timothy 4:12

♥ I am humble. I do not consider myself better than others. Philippians 2:3

♥ I serve others just as Jesus served the world. Matthew 20:25-28

♥ I have brotherly affection for those I serve. Romans 12:9-13

♥ I will not grow weary of doing good for those I serve. Galatians 6:9

♥ I look out for the interests of others. Philippians 2:4

♥ I work for the glory of Jehovah, not man. 2 Corinthians 9:6-7

♥ I treat others the way I would want to be treated. Luke 6:31

♥ Jehovah gives me wisdom to lead. James 1:5-6

♥ I am a faithful servant of what I have been given. Matthew 25:21

♥ I am a cheerful giver. 2 Corinthians 9:6-7

♥ I speak up for those who can't speak for themselves. Proverbs 31:8-9

♥ I lead with enthusiasm and energy. Romans 12:8

♥ I serve with joy. Hebrews 13:17

My Affirmations

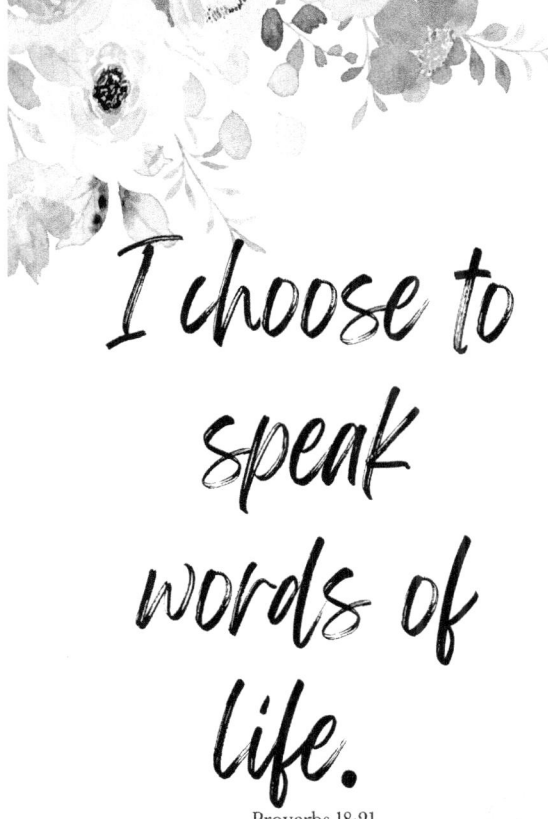

I choose to speak words of life.

Proverbs 18:21

Thirteen

Affirmations for Self-Control

Do you have trouble controlling your impulses? If so, this is another area you can use biblical affirmations to change your mindset.

Say these affirmations aloud:

♥ The Holy Spirit has gifted me with self-control. Galatians 5:22-23

♥ I discipline my body and have it under complete control. 1 Corinthians 9:24-27

♥ The grace of Jehovah teaches me self-control. Titus 2:11-14

♥ I am in control of my words and my anger. James 1:19

♥ I am wise. I am in control of my emotions. Proverbs 29:11

♥ The Lord has set a guard over my mouth. I do not speak unkind words. Psalm 141:3

♥ I use my words wisely. I choose to speak words of life. Proverbs 18:21

♥ I am prudent. I can ignore an insult. Proverbs 12:16

♥ I will not avenge myself. Vengeance belongs to Jehovah. Romans 12:19

♥ I will abstain from every form of evil. 1 Thessalonians 5:22

♥ Sin does not reign in my body. Romans 6:12

♥ I walk by the Spirit, not by the flesh. Galatians 5:16-17

♥ I do not speak careless words. Matthew 12:36

My Affirmations

I walk by faith, not by sight.

2 Corinthians 5:7

Fourteen

Affirmations to Encourage Your Faith

As Christian women, we have to walk worthy of our calling (Ephesians 4:1). It is therefore important for us to improve our faith. We can do that by studying the Bible and seeking to know more about Jehovah. The better we know Him, the more we will love Him. We should also speak words of life and power so that our faith will grow.

The affirmations in this section encourage you to exercise your faith.

- ♥ I walk by faith, not by sight. 2 Corinthians 5:7

- ♥ My faith pleases Jehovah. Hebrews 11:6

- ♥ I stand firm in the faith. 1 Corinthians 16:13

- ♥ I live by faith. Romans 1:17

- ♥ My prayers are answered because my faith in Jesus is strong. Mark 11:24

- ♥ I believe, Lord. Help my unbelief. Mark 9:24

- ♥ My faith is increasing. Luke 17:5

- ♥ I am justified[3] by my faith in Christ. Romans 5:1

- ♥ I abide in Christ and He in me. I will bear much fruit. John 15:4

- ♥ I hold fast to the confession of my faith. I do not waver. Hebrews 10:23

- ♥ Jehovah is my strength. He gives me victory. Exodus 15:2

---

[3] Justified means to be declared or made righteous in the sight of God. (Oxford English Dictionary)

My Affirmations

I am in good health.

3 John 1:2

Fifteen

Affirmations for Healing/Health

Our health is of key importance if we're going to accomplish the work God has given us. It's for this reason the enemy sometimes attack our health. He knows that if we're sick, we can't do the work we're called to do. As you seek to affirm yourself in this area, I want you to remember that healing is not always physical.

Our spiritual health is more important than the physical and sometimes God chooses not to heal our physical ailments so we will remain in His presence (2 Corinthians 12:8-10).

Use the affirmations in this section to encourage yourself in matters of health and healing.

♥ I am healed because Jehovah has healed me. Jeremiah 17:14

♥ I am in good health. It is well with my soul. 3 John 1:2

- ♥ I have joy in my heart. Proverbs 17:22

- ♥ I have abundant life in Christ. John 10:10

- ♥ I am healed. My faith in Jesus has made me well. Mark 5:34

- ♥ I will rejoice in the Lord. Philippians 4:4

- ♥ Jehovah's grace is sufficient for me. My weakness is made perfect in His strength. 2 Corinthians 12:9

- ♥ I am jubilant[4] with joy. Psalm 68:3

---

[4] Jubilant means to have a feeling or expressing great happiness and triumph. (Oxford English Dictionary)

My Affirmations

Jehovah will establish the work of my hands.

Psalm 90:17

Sixteen

Choose the Positive

Our Heavenly Father loves us, so much so, He sent His Son from heaven to die for our sins (Jchn 3:15-16). When we sinned, He offered us grace and the hope of eternal life through Jesus, His Son. His Word has many positive words of affirmation for us.

From Genesis to Revelation, the Bible tells us about Jehovah's love for humanity. He's holding out His hand to us today, offering mercy and love. We are His children (Hebrews 11:5-6). We are his sons and daughters. I am the daughter of the Most High Jehovah. So are you.

Jehovah set us apart from the world so that we can be priests before Him. He crowned us with salvation and called us royal (1 Peter 2:9).

My sister-in-Christ, I encourage you to choose biblical affirmations to decree over your life. You'll be glad you did.

A Prayer of Biblical Affirmation

Abba Father, I come to You today because I want You to speak truth into my life. I recognize that sometimes the things I tell myself do not reflect the truth that comes from You.

Help me to not only speak good things over my life but to also believe only those things that line up with Your word. In Jesus' name I pray, Amen.

Author's Note

Thank you for reading this book of affirmations for Christian women. The words we speak really do have the power to speak life or death into our lives and those of the people around us, so speak life, my sister.

If you enjoyed this book, please consider leaving a short review online. Even a short sentence is enough to bring this book to the attention of other readers who need it.

Stay empowered, sister-in-Christ!

About the Author

Aminata Coote is a Christian author and blogger. She is passionate about teaching others how to study the Bible. She is a wife, mother, author, and follower of Jesus Christ who encourages women to spend time with God and root their identities in Christ so they'll be able to focus on running the race God has set before them.

She is the author of multiple books including How to Find Your Gratitude Attitude and The Book of Haggai Bible Study Workbook.

Connect with Aminata on her website: https://www.hebrews12endurance.com/ or @AminataCoote on Instagram or Facebook.

Printed in Great Britain
by Amazon